ACANTHUS PRESS REPRINT SERIES
THE 20TH CENTURY: LANDMARKS IN DESIGN

VOLUME

ELY JACQUES KAHN NEW YORK ARCHITECT

ELY JACQUES KAHN

New York Architect

With an
Introduction & a List of Works
Designed Between the Wars

by

Françoise Bollack & Tom Killian

ACANTHUS PRESS, NEW YORK 1995

Library of Congress Cataloging-in-Publication Data

Ely Jacques Kahn: New York Architect/ with an introduction and list of works
designed between the wars, by Françoise Bollack and Tom Killian.
    p.   cm.– (Acanthus reprint series. The 20th century–landmarks in design;
v. 4) Originally published: New York: Whittlesey House, 1931, in series.
Includes index.
ISBN 0-926494-04-X: $25.00

1. Kahn, Ely Jacques, 1884-1972–Catalogs. I. Bollack, Françoise Astrong.
II. Killian, Tom. III. Title. IV. Series: Acanthus Press reprint series: 20th
century, landmarks in design; v. 4.
NA737.K3A4   1995
720'.92–dc20   94-41202
                                                                   CIP

*R*eprinted by: Acanthus Press

54 West 21st Street, New York, NY 10010

Tel 212 463 0750

Fax 212 463 0752

Printed in the USA

INTRODUCTION

ELY JACQUES KAHN was one of the most prominent commercial architects in New York in the late 1920s—engagingly described by Allene Talmey in the New Yorker (11 Apr. 1931):

> ...the blue book of architecture and the Social Register are still one, yet Hood, Ely Jacques Kahn and Ralph Walker, the three little Napoleons of architecture are only in the telephone book. They are three little men who build tall buildings, and who probably take into their offices more business than any other architect in the city. . . They are constantly publicized, interviewed, quoted. They dash to Boston. They race to Chicago. They have a glorious time.
>
> The fine old gentlemen in their fine old offices distend their nostrils slightly ...[1]

Their rivals, the younger adherents of the International Style, led by Philip Johnson, scorned them as merely commercial, merely instruments of dirty business (dirty because business). This International Style triumphed after the Second World War (after 1945) with a somehow "clean" commercialism, part of a *new world,* the difference being that the architectural solutions were those invented as a part of a new Utopia: the clean curtain wall, the rational plans appealing to the new generation of businessmen—*out with the old, in with the new.*

The three Napoleons, as well as their lesser known colleagues, were forgotten.

But when we think of New York the strongest image is not Lever House nor the other curtain-walled pure forms. We are fascinated by the Chrysler building and Rockefeller Center—the "Speaking Architecture" of around 1930. Like King Kong we are drawn to the Empire State building.

Kahn designed only a few such towers, notably the Squibb Building, 111 John Street and 1441 Broadway. Most of his clients needed lower blocks, with large floors for their manufacturing enterprises. Kahn's talent, what set him apart, was his savage decoration (based on Mexican and American Indian motifs), his use of color against the sky (today seen most prominently in his 2 Park Avenue Building) and the design of his public spaces, using a personal palette of ornament (today best seen in the lobby of the Film Center building.)

Savage and vigorous but fine, Kahn's was a spirited and inventive solution to the difficult and delicate question of modern speech—modern because it was made by modern tools and modern workmen, modern because it addressed itself to modern Americans in 1930.

Of course this style has its sources, ancient (the savage mentioned above) and modern (Paris, c. 1925).

Perhaps none of Kahn's colleagues—a skillful and adventurous bunch—was quite his match in this specific talent, an idea mentioned by Cheney in his *New World Architecture*, 1930:

> Ely Jacques Kahn has, indeed, felt his way toward a severe flowering of decoration on a half dozen notable of New York business towers. There is no Viennese lightness here, no attempt to lighten or make elegant or graceful what is essentially heavy, sturdy, business-like. ...The point is that here is an elaboration of architecture that grew out of the actual new way of building, that was not thought of at all, separately, before the place for it was there, to be filled. That is the beginning point of the only honest kind of style.[2]

And today, how does this strike us? We have both the work of the "little Napoleons" and the clean abstract forms built after 1945.

With hindsight we see something not discussed in 1930, nor in 1950. Then the hope was for a *tabula rasa*, a clean slate: well separated towers connected by expressways, a *Rational* City, free of congestion—what Jane Jacobs in *The Death and Life of Great American Cities* called "an ideal of order and gentility so simple it could be engraved on the head of a pin." "This is not the rebuilding of cities. This is the sacking of cities." Jacobs did not see existing cities as chaotic but rather as having "a most intricate and unique order" and she made us see this order.

We see the newness of Kahn's (and his colleagues') work, its invention of appropriate forms, appropriate decorations, for the modern city, but we see also its continuity with the traditional city. Their buildings were not pure forms, but rather blocks modified, molded to fit into the existing context. They completed the city, giving this city of merchants a solid, savage presence. One cannot imagine New York, the Metropolis, without this architecture.

■ ■ ■

When Ely Jacques Kahn was in his late thirties, he became a partner in the firm of Buchman & Fox; the firm was renamed Buchman & Kahn around 1920 and produced work under this name until 1930. Kahn took over the firm that year, designing under his own name "Ely Jacques Kahn Architects" sometimes also publishing or filing at the building department under "The Firm of Ely Jacques Kahn."

Before 1926 Buchman & Kahn produced competent, solid buildings. The Hospital for Joint Diseases (1925), the Jay Thorpe Building (1921), and The Bonwit Teller Company Building (1911, at the south-east corner of Fifth Avenue and 38th Street), all still standing, are good examples. The fact that these commissions were mostly commercial—manufacturing and industrial—might well have been a liberation rather than a hindrance to Kahn's talent:

> ...and where likewise the monumental building disdainfully avoids variation
> from precedent, the industrial structure sails merrily into experiment.[3]

From the mid-1920s to the New York World's Fair in 1939-40 Ely Jacques Kahn, in the fertile environment of New York City, produced his best work, searching for solutions to the programs of the time—the large manufacturing building in the city and the tall setback office building—and developing his own style of architecture for Gotham City. Let us try to trace his evolution from the mid-twenties, when he had just turned 40, to 1930, the year when he designed two of his greatest buildings, the Holland Plaza Building and 136 East 57th Street (both still standing).

The Arsenal Building (1925, 7th Avenue and 35th Street) and the Furniture Exchange Building (1926, 200 Lexington Avenue, between 32nd and 33rd Street) experiment with a bolder, coarser, decorative vocabulary than Buchman & Kahn had been using up to this point.

The Arsenal has a four-story base on which sits an eleven-story building block crowned by a machicolated cornice where windows alternate with giant masonry corbels. On top of this main block sit two other setback blocks, each terminated by a less elaborate machicolated cornice. Although the whole building has a raw energy, there is little vertical integration of all the elements. It uses the basic scheme that Buchman & Fox and Buchman & Kahn had used: a relatively plain building resting on a two- to four-story base, articulated with various types of rustications, crowned by an ornamented top.

With the Ed. Pinaud Factory (1927, 214 East 21st Street, still standing), a small manufacturing building, Ely Jacques Kahn designed a perfectly integrated building. He gives to this urbane factory a facade with a lively texture perfectly controlled by a monumental classical scheme. A four-story giant "loggia" characterized by very large glazed openings, is framed left and right by a bay where solid masonry predominates. The top story is a new form of cornice—partly machicolations, partly rustications—and is brought into perfect harmony with the rest of the facade. The whole structure seems to be tightly woven and held in equilibrium by the surface of the wall itself. This is quite a departure from the Jay Thorpe or Arsenal buildings, where the body of each building seems to be an inert mass—a lull—between the articulations of the base and the top.

The Pinaud Factory scheme is one that Kahn uses and develops in larger structures such as 2 Park Avenue (1927), the United States Appraisers Building (1928), 42 West 39th Street (1928) and the Film Center (1929)—all still standing. His design for 2 Park Avenue uses color to articulate the facade with an unprecedented vigor—and to our knowledge never repeated, even in Kahn's own work. In this period Kahn writes extensively about the need to develop ornament which is appropriate to the role it plays in the building:

> The scale and mass of the ornament will be delicate or coarse in proportion to its proximity to the eye and be dependent on the material, whether bronze, stone, concrete or brick.[4]

He uses color to supplement, and maybe replace, the play of light and shadow that traditional ornament depends upon for its readability.

> Flat surfaces take the place of the obsolete cornices and finally color in surfaces, in proportion to the distance from the observer, mark the accents that the artist desires.[5]

> The possibilities of strong contrasts of colors, eliminating futile carving and the crockets, pinnacles and similar appendages of the early skyscraper, are unlimited.... The dream of a colored city, buildings in harmonious tones making great masses of beautiful pattern, may be less of a vision if the enterprising city developer suspects the result. There is evident economy of effort in the application of color in lieu of carved decoration that cannot be seen...[6]

The Film Center, a thirteen-story building occupying a full block front on 9th Avenue between 44th and 45th street uses, fundamentally, the same parti: massive ends frame a more open center brought together at the top by bold articulations—not a cornice any more but rather a combination of vigorous horizontal rustications at the building's corners and monumental keystones in between. Integration of the three registers of the building (base, middle and top) is achieved by transitional zones between each register where elements of both areas are meshed. This design was developed in the U.S. Appraisers Building and at 42-44 West 39th Street, using what was to become one of Art Deco's favorite schemes—a clearly articulated differentiation between the building's center and its edges, along with a design of the exterior wall where horizontal and vertical elements are woven and rewoven throughout the facade to achieve a particular emphasis.

The Film Center lobby dazzles with its showy, unrestrained and riotous use of color and shape: Frank Lloyd Wright, Arts and Crafts and Precolumbian architecture are all present here. The colored glass mosaics, the terrazzo, the brass decorative elements, the gusto with which the Architect "sails merrily into experiment" give the space a buoyant feel, as if an impish Mayan God were looking at us through the shimmering wall surface, ready to play tricks. In Kahn's own words:

> When we discuss our classics, and let no facetious note enter here, are not Cambodia, China, Mexico, Peru, Tibet also our cultural heritage? Would it not be far more entertaining to see the amazing wood carvings of the New Zealand primitives than an everlasting rewarming of New England.[7]

In designing a tall structure in the 1920s, the key problem for the Architect was how to comply with the setback requirements of the New York City zoning law while designing a building which was more than a pile of stacked boxes and still provide a client with the largest possible floor. With the Indemnity Building (also called the Insurance Building, 1928-29, 111 John Street; still standing), Ely Jacques Kahn continues to use classical principles to bring a recognizable order to the John Street facade where the main entrance is located, in spite of the different setback requirements governing Cliff Street on the west and Pearl Street on the east.

The design establishes an apparent bilateral symmetry above the three-story base through the use of vertical piers in the center. Through a continuous process of recentering, supported by the use of "dormers" whose location shifts with each setback, these vertical piers create the illusion of symmetry through most of the building's height. At the top, where the tower emerges, the vertical ribs take over to finally become the perfect center of a simple square tower. The interlocked massing of the building is held together by the design and detailing of the exterior wall, continuing a development started at the Pinaud factory. Horizontal brick bands and major and minor verticals (see for example the small vertical accents in the window spandrels located between the vertical piers) keep the surface in tension: it is as if all the strands are always there just below the surface but weave in and out of view to produce the desired emphasis. Of his interest in this period, Kahn was to say later "I was thinking of the texture of fabric"[8]

A comparison of this design with the slightly earlier Insurance Center (1926-27, 80 John Street; still standing) reveals Kahn's development within the particularly rich architectural climate of the time in New York City.

In contrast to the highly articulated massing of the Indemnity Building, the design of the Holland Plaza Building (1930, Canal and Varick; still standing), one of Kahn's masterpieces, inspires awe through its sheer simplicity. It is a fifteen-story manufacturing structure with nine truck loading bays on Watts Street and twelve freight elevators in addition to its ten passenger elevators. The building has a two-story base and, on Canal Street, a wall rising uninterrupted to a boldly rusticated top floor wrapping around the whole structure. The building is striking for its use of monumental pilasters to delineate the center of each facade and the unique design of its window wall; here the surface becomes a web, a grid where horizontal and vertical forces are in equilibrium. The points of elaboration in the brickwork are located at the intersection of the horizontal spandrels and of the vertical piers. This neutral field of masonry and glass extends on all facades to the building's corners, framing the loggias. The boldness of such a simple, monumental design and the economy of means with which it is carried out make this building one of the masterpieces of industrial architecture and one of Kahn's best buildings.

The lobby, which seems to have been every bit as astounding as that of the Film Center, has sadly been altered. From the photographs it appears to bear some resemblance to the lobby of 259–263 Fifth Avenue, which is fortunately still extant: one can only hope that it will be rediscovered or restored at some point.

One cannot help but feel that the design for the Holland Plaza Building was an important source for the design of the small office building at 136 East 57th Street (1930–31, south-east corner of 57th Street and Lexington Avenue; still standing). With this building Kahn comes closest to meeting his ambition of achieving Modern architecture's ideal of simplification, elision and gridding, but the design is nonetheless tempered by memory of the Classical. The building appears smaller than it actually is, due to the use of masonry openings grouping two stories. Rising over a two-story limestone base, delicate horizontal rustications give the gridded brick curtain wall a fine, regular texture. The building is simple, compact and calm. Here, as at the Holland Plaza Building, Kahn has achieved full mastery of his Art and gives form, without apologies, to the architectural problem of his time—stated in one form or another in numerous articles published between 1926 and 1930 (the date of the building's design):

> The theory of the modern designer consists very simply in the answering of a problem; whether the task be the painting of a picture, the design of a chair, the writing of a book, the result should be no other than an honest solution.[9]

and finally...

> The beauty of a plain surface, relieved in whatever way the artist may
> desire, is the ideal. After all there is no new principle involved, for
> through all time the same theory has dominated those works that
> remain to us as masterpieces. The modernist uses his material so as to
> make it beautiful in itself. Marble, glass, fabrics, wood, do not need
> applied decoration to glorify their beauty or texture. The problem, sim-
> plifying itself to a matter of form, contrast or proper use of material,
> now demands particular study.[10]

■ ■ ■

The list of buildings which follows is as comprehensive as we have been able
to make it for the period of 1918 to 1941; however it is highly probable that the
list is not exhaustive. Work outside of New York City (therefore not filed at the
New York City Building Department), unpublished at the time, and whose drawings are still in private hands, is unlikely to be listed. We can only hope that
there are few such examples.

The period covered by the list is greater than the period covered by the first
edition of *Contemporary American Architects: Ely Jacques Kahn*. In that book
Kahn dates his buildings by their construction date: for example the Glen Oaks
Country Club is dated 1929, whereas drawings in the Avery Library Archive
bear the date 1928-29. The date we use is, in general, the date the building was
designed or, at times, the date at which the project was filed. When more than
one year is stated (for example 1930-32), we believe the first date is when the
design was started (in our example 1930) and the second date indicates when
the building was built (in our example 1932). Some works, designated by the
name of the client, or dates are not easy to clarify. Kahn had many long-term,
repeat clients: for example, the Ruppert family, for whose brewery Buchman &

Kahn had designed a substantial alteration, hired Ely Jacques Kahn in 1939 to design a Garden Pavilion for the New York World's Fair. Kahn also designed renovations or alterations for many of his own buildings (e.g. 2 Park Avenue and 267 Fifth Avenue). In 1911 Buchman & Kahn designed a building for Bonwit Teller on the south-east corner of Fifth Avenue and 38th Street, then later did a substantial renovation of Bonwit's new Fifth Avenue store (itself designed by Warren & Wetmore); the Jay Thorpe building, designed by Buchman & Kahn, was expanded by Ely Jacques Kahn.

By virtue of this repeat business, we can paint an enviable picture of an architectural practice made up of a substantial number of satisfied, appreciative clients who tended to come back to "the family architect", so to speak, when they needed to build again.

NEW YORK, 1995   FRANÇOISE BOLLACK & TOM KILLIAN

Notes:
1. Quoted by Robert A.M. Stern in *Raymond Hood*.
2. *The New World Architecture*, p. 227.
3. *Contemporary American Architects: Ely Jacques Kahn* [CAA], p. 16 "On the Development of the Industrial Buildings"; 1929.
4. *CAA* p. 20 "On Decoration and Ornament"; 1929.
5. *CAA* p. 21 "On Decoration and Ornament"; 1929.
6. *CAA* p. 23 "On the Use of Color"; 1928.
7. *The American Architect*; April 1930.
8. Ely Jacques Kahn's unpublished autobiography; Avery Architecture Library Archive.
9. *CAA* p. 14 "On what is Modern"; 1930.
10 *CAA* p. 10 "On the Present American Predicament"; 1929.

The sources for the list of buildings are:

AIA Guide to New York City by Elliot Willenski & Norval White New York: Harcourt Brace Jovanovich Publishers. Third Edition, 1988.

The Architectural Forum

Art Deco Architecture in New York, 1920–1940 by Don Vlack.
New York, Harper & Row, 1974.

Avery Architecture Library Archive
Avery Architecture Library of Columbia Univerisity, New York.

Contemporary American Architects–Ely Jacques Kahn [referenced as CAA in the list]. New York, Whittelsey House, 1931.

Creative Art magazine

Dawn of a New Day – The New York World's Fair, 1939/40
Catalogue of an exhibition at The Queens Museum; Helen A. Harrison, Guest Curator. New York, New York University Press, 1980

Forging a Metropolis – Walking Tours of Lower Manhattan Architecture
Published in conjunction with the exhibition "Forging a Metropolis: Architecture of Lower Manhattan" presented at the Whitney Museum of American Art, Downtown at Federal Plaza, August 8-October 19, 1990. © 1990 Whitney Museum of American Art.

"Lower Manhattan Survey Report"
Prepared for the Lower Manhattan Cultural Council ©
by Andrew Dolkart-Fall 1987

Municipal Archive
Dockets of applications to the New York City building department for new buildings and alterations kept at the Municipal Archive.

The New World Architecture
by Sheldon Cheney. New York, Longmans, Green, 1930.

New York 1930: Architecture and Urbanism Between The Two World Wars by Robert A. M. Stern, Gregory Gilmartin, and Thomas Mellins.
New York, Rizzoli International Publications, 1987.

The New York World's Fair, 1939/40, In 155 Photographs by Richard Wurts and Others. Section, Arrangement and Text by Stanley Applebaum. New York, Dover Publications, Inc., 1977.

"The New York World's Fair in Pictures"
Long Island City, NY, Quality Novelty Company Inc., 1939
(Views of the New York World's Fair published at the time of the Fair)

Pencil Points magazine

Raymond Hood by Robert A.M. Stern. New York, Rizzoli, 1982.

Skyscraper Style–Art Deco New York by Cervin Robinson & Rosemarie Haag Bletter. New York, Oxford University Press, 1975.

ELY JACQUES KAHN – LIST OF WORKS DESIGNED BETWEEN THE TWO WORLD WARS

by Françoise Bollack & Tom Killian

Within the list, a few buildings are marked with a star indicating that they seem, to the authors, to be the best (at least in their present state in 1995) in exemplifying Kahn's particular talent as well as being beautiful.

1918   RESIDENCE OF MR. ELY JACQUES KAHN
Elmsford, NY.
CAA p. 30.

1919   LEHN & FINK BUILDING
Northeast Corner of Greenwich & Morton Streets, NYC
Buchman & Kahn; Avery Library Archive - Item N⁰K-28

1919   GARAGE – ESTATE OF MR. JOSEPH PLAUT
Elmsford, NY
CAA p. 31.

1919   GARAGE – ESTATE OF MR. HERMAN YOUNKER
Elmsford, NY.
CAA p. 32.

1919   ZIMMERMAN SAXE AND ZIMMERMAN ASSOCIATES
5th Avenue & 25th Street, NYC
CAA p. 33; NY 1930 p.59

1919   OPPENHEIM-COLLINS & COMPANY BUILDING & SUBSEQUENT
ALTERATIONS
1924/1928   527-529 Penn Avenue, Pittsburgh, PA.
Buchman & Kahn; Avery Library Archive - Item K31

1919-21   BUILDING AT 7TH AVENUE & 36TH STREET (SOUTH-EAST CORNER), NYC
Buchman & Kahn; Avery Library Archive - Item N⁰K-29

1919-22   BORDEN BUILDING
Madison Avenue & 45th Street, (Southwest Corner), NYC
Buchman & Kahn; Avery Library Archive - Item N⁰K-30
NY 1930 p. 553 in the text

1920-21   BUILDING FOR STEIGER-VEDDER COMPANY
Main & Pratt Streets, (Northwest Corner), Hartford, CT.
Buchman & Fox; Buchman & Kahn; Avery Library Archive - Item N⁰K-32

1921   ALTERATIONS TO EDWIN HARRIS RESIDENCE
314 West 82nd Street, NYC
Buchman & Kahn; Avery Library Archive - Item N⁰K-33

1926   LOFT BUILDING AT 247 WEST 35TH STREET, NYC
        (Between 7th & 8th Avenues)
        Buchman & Kahn; Avery Library Archive - Item NºK-51

1926   BUILDING AT 58-60 BROAD STREET, NYC
        Buchman & Kahn; Avery Library Archive - Item NºK-52

1926   PARK/MURRAY CORPORATION BUILDING
        9-15 Park Place and 8-12 Murray Street, NYC
        Still standing – entry on Murray Street extant, entry on Park Place altered.
        Buchman & Kahn; Avery Library Archive - Item NºK-53
        NY 1930 p. 556 in the text.

1926   BUILDING AT 269-271 MADISON AVENUE, NYC
        Buchman & Kahn; Avery Library Archive - Item NºK-54

1926-28 LEFCOURT EXCHANGE BUILDING
        Corner of Broad & Beaver Streets, NYC
        Buchman & Kahn; Avery Library Archive - Item NºK-55

1926   BUILDING AT 65 WEST 37TH STREET, NYC
        Buchman & Kahn; CAA pp. 46-47; NY 1930 illustrated on p. 560

1926   APARTMENT FOR VICTOR RIESENFELD
        1050 Park Avenue, NYC
        Ely Jacques Kahn; NY 1930 p. 466 in the text

1926-27 INSURANCE CENTER BUILDING
        80 John Street, NYC
        Buchman & Kahn; CAA p. 52-53; Skyscraper Style #3 and model
        photograph on p. 14; NY 1930 p. 555 in the text;
        "Lower Manhattan" item # 92; Forging a Metropolis p. 69

1926-28 LEFCOURT STATE BUILDING
        1375 Broadway, NYC. Northwest Corner of Broadway and 37th Street.
        Buchman & Kahn; Avery Library Archive - Item NºK-61
        CAA p. 63 detail of top only.; Art Deco Architecture listed on p. 154

1926-28 BUILDING AT NUMBER TWO PARK AVENUE, NYC ✶
        Buchman & Kahn; Avery Library Archive - Item NºK-64
        1927 in CAA pp. 56 through 61; Skyscraper Style, # 6 and color photograph;
        Art Deco Architecture Figure #8 p. 15; NY 1930 illustration on p. 560,
        in the text p. 555-6; Creative Art December 1929: article by
        E.J. Kahn, photograph of bronze entrance.
1936   Alteration by Ely Jacques Kahn
1964   Remodeling by Kahn & Jacobs

1927   MAUSOLEUM FOR H. GOLDMAN,
        Rodeph Sholom Congregation Cemetery, Queens, NY
        Buchman & Kahn; Avery Library Archive - Item NºK-56

1927 RUTLEY'S RESTAURANT
Broadway at 40th Street, NYC
Buchman & Kahn; CAA p. 49

1927 BUILDING AT 247 WEST 35TH STREET, NYC
Buchman & Kahn; CAA p. 50, entrance view only

1927 ED. PINAUD FACTORY ✳
214 East 21st Street, NYC
Buchman & Kahn; CAA p. 51; NY 1930 illustrated on p. 559;
Architectural Forum September 1929; perspective drawing p. 275, photo
p. 277-278.

1927-28 INTERNATIONAL TELEPHONE AND TELEGRAPH BUILDING
67 Broad Street (at Broad, Beaver and S. William Streets), NYC
Buchman & Kahn ;CAA p. 54-55; "Lower Manhattan" #55;
Forging a Metropolis p. 59.

1927 BERGDORF GOODMAN ✳
1 West 57th Street, NYC
(Facade at entrance on Fifth Avenue altered.)
Buchman & Kahn; Avery Library Archive - Item N°K-57
CAA p. 62; AIA Guide, p. 280; NY 1930 in text p. 318

1927 UNITED APPRAISERS BUILDING
at Varick, King & Houston Streets, NYC
Buchman & Kahn; Avery Library Archive - Item N°K- 58
CAA p. 68 through 70; Architectural Forum September 1929 in an article
by E.J.Kahn, pp. 273, 274 and 276

1927 FEDERATION BUILDING
67-71 West 47th Street, NYC
Buchman & Kahn; Avery Library Archive - Item N°K- 59
1928 in CAA p. 72-73

1927-28 GLEN OAKS GOLF & COUNTRY CLUB
Great Neck, Long Island, NY
Buchman & Kahn; Avery Library Archive - Item N°K-60; CAA p. 82-83

1927 LUDWIG BAUMAN & COMPANY BUILDING
at Hoyt, Livingston & Schermerhorn Streets, Brooklyn, NY.
1935 Buchman & Kahn; Ely Jacques Kahn; Avery Library Archive - Item N°K-62

1927 GRAND CENTRAL BUILDING ✳
42-50 West 39th Street, NYC
Buchman & Kahn; Avery Library Archive - Item N°K-63;
CAA p. 66-67; Skyscraper Style #7, color photograph.
1940 Remodeling by Kahn & Jacobs

1928-30 REMODELING OF BONWIT TELLER
        5th Avenue (Northeast Corner of 56 Street.), NYC
        Demolished. Ely Jacques Kahn; CAA pp. 100-101; NY 1930 illustrated
        on p. 316; Skyscraper Style # 25

   1929 56TH STREET ADDITION TO JAY THORPE BUILDING
        Buchman & Kahn; CAA p. 35; NY 1930 p. 363 in the text.

   1929 METROPOLITAN MUSEUM OF ART EXHIBIT – GARDEN SEAT AND TABLE
        Ely Jacques Kahn. CAA p. 76; Pencil Points March 1929, Supplement
        108, photograph p. 199 & description by E.J. Kahn on p. 108;
        Metropolitan Museum of Art exhibit - Bath and Dressing Room; CAA p. 77

   1929 APARTMENT OF MRS. ALFRED L. ROSE, NYC
        Ely Jacques Kahn. CAA p. 79, Detail only. NY 1930 illustrated on p. 465

   1929 LIBRARY FOR CHARLES J. LIEBMAN ESQ.
        907 Fifth Avenue, NYC
        Ely Jacques Kahn. CAA p. 93; NY 1930 p. 466 in the text and
        illustrated on p. 463

   1929 ADLER BUILDING
        530 7th Avenue (Southwest Corner of 39th Street), NYC
        Buchman & Kahn; Avery Library Archive - Item NºK-75; CAA p. 84
   1966 Remodeling by Kahn & Jacobs

   1929 YARDLEY AND COMPANY LTD.
        452 Fifth Avenue, NYC
        Buchman & Kahn; CAA p. 85 (interior); NY 1930 in the text on p. 298.

   1929 ALLIED ARTS BUILDING ✱
        304 East 45th Street, NYC
        Buchman & Kahn; CAA p. 86; Skyscraper Style# 23; Art Deco Architecture
        listed on p. 152

   1929 BOWKER BUILDING
        415 Park Avenue South (Southeast Corner of 29th Street & Park), NYC
        Ely Jacques Kahn; AIA Guide p. 194

   1929 VAN CLEEF AND ARPELS, JEWELERS
        671 Fifth Avenue at 53rd Street, NYC
        Buchman & Kahn; CAA Interior p. 89, NY 1930 in the text p. 298

1929-30 ROLLS ROYCE BUILDING ✱
        32-34 East 57th Street, NYC
        Buchman & Kahn; Avery Library Archive - Item NºK-70

1929-30 BROADMOOR PHARMACY IN LEFCOURT COLONIAL BUILDING, NYC
        Southeast Corner of Madison Avenue and East 41st Street.
        Ely Jacques Kahn; Avery Library Archive - Item NºK-73
        NY 1930 p. 306 in the text.

[XXII]

1929-30 SQUIBB BUILDING ✶
          5th Avenue at 58th Street (Southeast Corner), NYC
          Buchman & Kahn; Ely Jacques Kahn & Sherley W. Morgan;
          Avery Library Archive - Item N°K-74
          CAA pp. 94 through 99; NY 1930 p. 557-58 in the text,
          illustrated pp. 200, 220, 512, 563 and on the cover; AIA Guide p. 281;
          Art Deco Architecture illustration Figure 98; Skyscraper Style #40.
1951, 1953 Remodeling by Kahn & Jacobs
     1983 Base substantially altered by Hammond, Beebe and Babka.

1929-31 120 WALL STREET BUILDING, NYC ✶
          Buchman & Kahn; Avery Library Archive - Item N°K-71
          CAA p. 87-88; NY 1930 p. 557 in the text and illustrated on pp. 600 and
          602; Art Deco Architecture illustration Figure 82 (Lobby) and listed on
          p. 153; "Lower Manhattan" item #48 (description and photo of entry)

1929-31 SEYMOUR A. STRAUSS MAUSOLEUM
          Mount Pleasant Cemetery, Hawthorne, NY.
          Buchman & Kahn; Avery Library Archive - Item N°K-72

1930-31 BRICKEN CASINO BUILDING
          1410 Broadway (Southeast Corner of 39th Street), NYC
          Buchman & Kahn; Ely Jacques Kahn; Avery Library Archive - Item N°K-77
          CAA pp. 102-105 and 107; Skyscraper Style # 80

   1930 DAILY COMMERCE BUILDING
          155 East 44th Street (Northwest Corner of Third Avenue & 44th Street), NYC
          Buchman & Kahn; Ely Jacques Kahn; Avery Library Archive - Item N°K-79
          CAA p. 114-116; Mailbox detail in CAA on p. 117;
          Skyscraper Style #84; NY 1930 p. 158 in the text.

   1930 HOLLAND PLAZA BUILDING ✶
          Canal and Varick Streets, NYC
          Buchman & Kahn; CAA p. 90-92, p. 119 (entrance). Art Deco
          Architecture, illustration Figure 81; NY 1930 illustrations on pp. 518 & 519

   1930 APARTMENT OF MRS. MAURICE S. BENJAMIN, NYC
          In The Beresford - 81st Street & Central Park West.
          Ely Jacques Kahn; CAA p. 98; NY 1930 in the text p. 466, illustrated p. 465.
          Progressive Architecture, June 1978, pp. 78-79 (photographs by Cervin Robinson.)

   1930 PROPOSED SKYSCRAPER
          Ely Jacques Kahn; NY 1930 illustrated on p. 561;
          Architectural Forum June 1930, p. 805 (plate 156).

1930-31 BUILDING AT 136 EAST 57TH STREET, NYC ✶
          (Southeast Corner of Lexington Avenue)
          Buchman & Kahn; Ely Jacques Kahn; Avery Library Archive - Item N°K-76
          CAA p. 112; NY 1930 illustrated on p. 56.

1930-31 BUILDING AT 1400 BROADWAY, NYC
          Northeast Corner of 38th Street
          Buchman & Kahn; Ely Jacques Kahn; Avery Library Archive - Item N°K-78
          CAA p. 109; *Skyscraper Style* # 81

1930-31 RICHARD HUDNUT BUILDING
          693-695 Fifth Avenue, NYC. Demolished.
          Ely Jacques Kahn & Eliel Saarinen; Avery Library Archive - Item N°K-81
          (Kahn credits the design of the facade to Saarinen in his unpublished
          autobiography kept in the Avery; Library Archive); CAA pp. 110-111;
          NY 1930 illustrated on p. 299

1930-31 CONTINENTAL BUILDING
          1450 Broadway (Southeast Corner of 41st Street), NYC
          Ely Jacques Kahn; Avery Library Archive - Item N°K-82
          CAA p. 108; *NY 1930* in the text p. 557; *Architectural Forum* June
          1930, pp. 795 & 796, perspective and construction data.

   1931 PARAMOUNT BUILDING WAREHOUSE
          521 West 43rd Street, NYC. CAA p. 106

   1931 745 FIFTH AVENUE, LERON LINGERIE AND LINEN
          CAA p. 113 (shop exterior)

   1931 WILLIAM R. ROSE MAUSOLEUM
          Woodland Cemetery, Queens, NY.
          Ely Jacques Kahn; Avery Library Archive - Item N°K-80

1934-36 OFFICES AND ALTERATIONS TO JACOB RUPPERT BREW HOUSE, NYC
          Third Avenue from 91st to 92nd Street. Demolished.
          Ely Jacques Kahn; Avery Library Archive - Item N°K-83; Municipal Archive

   1935 REMODELING OF 938 BROADWAY, NYC
          Ely Jacques Kahn; *AIA Guide* p. 188
          Note: this building still exists but is unrecognizable due to substantial
          alterations by Conklin and Rossant.

   1935 ALTERATIONS TO 530 & 550 7TH AVENUE, NYC
          (tunnel between the two buildings)
          Ely Jacques Kahn; Municipal Archive

   1936 FASHION SHOWROOM FOR HAZEL KOLIMAN
          NY 1930 p. 325 in the text.

   1936 ALTERATIONS TO 182-200 & 181-185 HUDSON STREET, NYC
          (tunnel between the two buildings)
          Ely Jacques Kahn; Municipal Archive

   1936 EXTENSION OF 42-50 WEST 39TH STREET, NYC
          Ely Jacques Kahn; Municipal Archive

■ ■ ■

CONTEMPORARY AMERICAN ARCHITECTS

CONTEMPORARY AMERICAN ARCHITECTS

ELY JACQUES KAHN

WHITTLESEY HOUSE

McGRAW-HILL BOOK COMPANY INC. - NEW YORK AND LONDON

1   9   3   1

Published by WHITTLESEY HOUSE

A DIVISION OF THE McGRAW-HILL BOOK COMPANY, INC.

New York and London

Printed in the United States of America by PRINTING SERVICE CORPORATION · *New York*

FOREWORD

PERHAPS THE ACADEMIC dissertations pertaining to architecture that emanate from non-professionals and a few architects have a value in stimulating thought among laymen, however confused such thought may be. These opinions and ideas should be discounted to a considerable extent because architecture is far beyond the realm of abstract speculation in that its manifestations in material forms involve many elements that are of a purely practical, utilitarian and financial nature, an understanding of which is acquired by experience only. Leadership in the development of architecture obtains in those architects who are in advance of the commonly accepted ideas and customs and who realize the necessity of correlating architecture with actual current requirements and with what their prophetical perceptions visualize as future requirements. It is interesting to note the dates atttached to the excerpts from the writings of Ely Jacques Kahn and relate them to the then current ideas and practices. Many of his ideas, as then expressed, are now accepted as correct and for that reason are a part of the true record of architectural development.

Appraisals of buildings to determine their real contribution to achitecture must include inquiries as to whether they "work",—fulfill their intended purpose,—and are sound financial projects. In both these respects the buildings designed by Mr. Kahn are successful and at the same time he has complied with all legal and economic requirements.

Architecture, when seriously undertaken, has a quality imparted to it by the personal attributes of the architect, and, knowing these, one's appraisal is rendered much easier and with better understanding. The more liberal, cultural and diversified these attributes, the more liberal, cultured and reasonable is the architect's attitude towards his professional work. The keen interest and understanding displayed by Mr. Kahn in music, painting, sculpture, literature, craftsmanship and cognate subjects, has a liberalizing and tolerant effect on his work. At no time, probably, was there a greater need than there is at present for leadership exempt from the influence of traditions which are not consonant with contemporary civilization. This is especially true of architecture. Mr. Kahn evidences in his work a freedom from old-established conventions that are common features of American architecture at this time, and in this he displays an unusual facility that is guided by a cultivated sense of discrimination, and a continuous growth that is essential to the evolution of a great architecture.

NEW YORK, 1931.   ARTHUR TAPPAN NORTH

ELY JACQUES KAHN

BORN NEW YORK CITY, *June 1, 1884; son of Jacques and Eugenie (Maximilian) Kahn. Columbia University, B.A., 1903; B.Arch., 1907; Architecte Diplomé par le Gouvernement Français, 1911.*

Professor of Design, Cornell University, 1915; lecturer on architecture, Metropolitan Museum of Art; instructor of design, New York University. Award in painting, Salon des Artistes Français, 1910; Prix Labarre, L'Ecole des Beaux Arts, 1911; one of Co-operating Committee of the Metropolitan Museum of Art's American Industrial Art Exhibition, 1929.

Member: Architectural League of New York; American Institute of Architects; Beaux Arts Society; Bund Deutscher Architekten, Berlin.

Mr. Kahn is an extensive reader of English, French and German literature; is interested in all phases of architecture and the allied arts and the craftsmanship of metals, textiles, glass and other related materials. To all of these he gives studious consideration whether it be the designing of a cosmetic compact or an important structure. His democratic manner, interested consideration of matters brought to his attention, tolerance for the views and opinions of others, and amiable disposition, cause him to be held in friendly regard and respect.

IN PRESENTING the following items, the author has preferred, rather than assume the rôle of interpreter, to allow the architect to speak for himself. The following paragraphs are excerpts from numerous articles Mr. Kahn has written at various times for art and architectural publications. In them he has clearly stated his views on design, materials and decoration in their relation not only to architecture but to all art where function and beauty are one.

The consistency of the philosophy contained in these statements, and his work as exemplified in the accompanying photographs, is so marked that it requires no further mention. Mr. Kahn has always been a true modernist in his appreciation of honesty in design and materials, in his ability to analyze the fundamentals of a problem and his power to enhance a frank expression of its solution. His interest in structure and decoration has led him to a very thorough study of the potentialities of new materials and their adaptability to modern usage; and entirely in keeping with his theory of experimentation he has used these materials in his practice and often led the way to their general acceptance.

As one would expect in every successful artist's work, there has been a steady growth in the development of Mr. Kahn's ideas, and it is with the intention of more clearly showing this growth that the photographs have been arranged in chronological order. That there should be a great diversity of solutions and executions among them agrees entirely with his conviction that function lies at the basis of all design, that each problem must be solved for itself alone, and that each solution must be an honest interpretation of that problem. In this regard, and particularly in these days of architectural specialization, it is interesting to note the variety of problems he has encountered. The list includes loft buildings, hospitals, restaurants, houses, office buildings, country clubs, warehouses, apartments, specialty shops, factories, department stores, numerous exhibitions and many designs for fabrics, mosaics, furniture, glass and metal craft of all kinds. Indeed, it seems clear that only an artist with a fundamental point of view and a thorough cultural background could approach and successfully solve problems as diverse as these.

OTTO JOHN TEEGEN

NEW YORK CITY, 1931

On the Present American Predicament

AMERICAN DESIGN in architecture maintains the last bulwark of classicism, if by that term one can refer to veneration of historic form rather than to profound knowledge of classic reasoning. What the clear mind of a Greek of the Periclean period might do, were it possible to present the modern problem to his attention, is interesting to consider. It is reasonable to assume that he would not exert himself to adapt the architecture of Rameses or the faded glories of Babylon. Much American energy is directed toward reproducing anything architectural that possesses an ancestor, whether it be Colonial, Romanesque, Greek, or what one will. The enthusiasm of the architect in discovering the existence of evidences of past performances of note is worthy, and much of the painstaking study and careful execution is admirable. How much of this mass of work actually indicates a sense of design or fitness, looking beyond the acquired technique as more or less mechanical, is another matter. Consider, for example, the typical American store. We have had English "shoppes,"—fake half-timber,—on Fifth Avenue; Italian palaces,—anything that admitted of a reasonable amount of rather indifferently executed decoration. Coincidentally, the mechanics of the store building were being developed. Maintaining the pace and intelligence of American industrial development, elevators, ventilation, shipping appurtenances, floors, fire control, details for the comfort and protection of the customers were studied, specified and installed with little resistance. The shell itself, the physical block, varied little except that the large stores increased in size and the smaller stores, primarily, in

[9]

luxury of equipment. The fault may be that of the architect, or it may possibly be due to the persistence of a myopic client, but, by and large, in proportion to the amount of work accomplished, it is difficult to refer with enthusiasm to many designs that stand close scrutiny.

Europe, quite naturally, had, and still has, its volume of mediocrity. Since 1900 the influence of the modern movement has been paramount, and together with the shock of a devastating war period and the lack of capital, the designers have struggled against obvious antagonism to a point where practically all of Europe is accepting the fact that something new has now to be acknowledged. The designers have realized that the work of the highly elaborate periods of the seventeenth and eighteenth centuries was done when labor was cheap and materials relatively inexpensive. The money available was in the hands of a few, and they could spend in a lordly and magnificent manner. The modern designer has to deal with a practical problem of material, probably quite different from what his ancestors faced. What is important is that the European public, as well as their designers, are aware of the situation.

Most of the quarrel with the old work is that it is burdened with applied decoration that has absolutely no significance to our generation. The beauty of a plain surface, relieved in whatever way the artist may desire, is the ideal. After all, there is no new principle involved, for through all time the same theory has dominated those works that remain to us as masterpieces. The modernist uses his material so as to make it beautiful in itself. Marble, glass, fabrics, wood, do not need applied decoration to glorify their beauty or texture. The problem, simplifying itself to a matter of form, contrast or proper use of material, now demands particular study.

The final analyses would seem to hold that the present mode requires the sensitive and minute study that the production of any simple form requires. The designer need not fear as to style, for most of the work that involves characteristically decorated forms based on geometric patterns is tiresome in its repetition and will not last. But the clarity of the new movement, is intelligence and its imaginative courage, may conceivably carry it far.

1929

. . .

ON THE PUBLIC'S CONTRIBUTION

THE FIRST REQUISITE is the stimulation of the owner to realize that experiment is the soul of a civilized being. As long as the client is smugly content with a third rate copy of the spurious antique, the designer has neither the opportunity nor the enthusiasm to sharpen his wits. The public must, itself, demand release from the heavy and deadly practice of copying. It will probably make mistakes and be human in making them, but it is inconceivable that any great influence can be exerted by a few men or a few intelligent clients while the bulk of the country rests placidly under spurious laurels, congratulating itself on its refined taste in knowing where to find questionable antiques and gloating over the odds and ends that Europe is glad to ship over at a price.

1930

ON WHAT IS MODERN

NOTHING IS MODERN other than that it represents its own time. The Greeks were quite as modern when they were building their homes and their temples and differed from their ancestors. The artists of the Renaissance were equally modern when they broke the rigid conventions of their day and inspired themselves from the great work of Rome and Greece. All through history we have experienced the same situation. Whenever a healthy group of men were working and were backed by an active and intelligent public, there came the inevitable break with some of the forms of the past. Whether these breaks were caused by developments of a practical nature—new methods of construction, new material, the use of electricity, central heating, or merely the result of a powerful force such as the dictum of Napoleon to refer back to the Roman Empire or Egypt, as sources of inspiration, the fact remains the same. There was a moment of resistance, annoyance at the discarding of comfortably accepted forms and the gradual evolution of a contemporary style.

We are faced today with a most curious situation. Europe for more than thirty years has been experimenting with the possibilities of a new expression in architecture, furniture, all of the details of present day life. Much of it has been bad, as would be natural in any new movement. What is to remain will be a small proportion of work that is based on sound design, good judgment, good taste. In America, the movement appeared as a request to accept a very radical conception of painting and sculpture, which has still failed to convince the American public. The skyscrapers developed their own forms through the force of circumstances and they alone have stood the test and are accepted as worthy efforts. In decoration, because there was none of the vigorous force that actuated the skyscraper builders, copies of European work appeared, much of it bad, a great deal of it entirely unrelated to American conditions or taste.

There is one consideration that is of major importance. If one is sincere in an admiration for any period, the Colonial, for example, let the individual realize that in the day when the originals were made men were designing, not copying. Problems were solved. The spirit, the charm, delicacy, the wit of the Colonial people can be invoked and if there is sufficient imagination available it is conceivable that even in these days furniture, fabrics, lighting fixtures, houses, may be produced that may be equally inspiring to another generation. There is no future, no life, in the absurd copies and senseless adaptations of Colonial kitchens to modern offices, the homes of virile women and men. Modernism has nothing whatsoever to do with the situation; the demand is for a rational interpretation of our own problems controlled by what good taste we possess. We have available materials, machines, opportunities that the world has never before seen. If we fail to create something of value in the experiment we can only blame our lack of ability and wait for another generation to show us the way. In copying there is complete failure, whether it be imitation of our own ancestors or modern Europe. Perhaps we are not capable as yet to perform, but when the public realizes the situation and demands something better the first step towards a modern and American style will have been made.

True modernism in design lies in solving each practical modern problem in the most direct and honest way. Whatever measure of beauty the resulting design may have is dependent upon this honesty and upon the personal attributes of the designer. Much depends upon his qualities of mind and spirit, upon his background; and his skill as an artist.

Approaching the subject in this way immediately relieves it of the confusion that prevails so generally; it reveals modernism as something more significant and worthy than a set of mannerisms or a collection of adaptable design motives to which a label has been affixed.

Lacking this understanding, many designers who think that they have gained freedom have merely changed masters. They are still doing imitative work, combining in various ways the forms and design motives that certain well-known contemporary designers prefer. They work from documents of what they understand as the Modern Style just as they have been in the habit of working from documents of the Classic, Mediaeval and Renaissance periods. Such a misconception of modernism is deadening.

Others, also lacking a true understanding of the matter, seem to think that freedom of expression in design lies in doing something different, arbitrarily and wilfully. They offer vagaries and eccentricities as a specious substitute for logically developed modern design. It is men of this class who have done most to discredit modernism. It is usually the work of some such unsound artist that is held up by the critics of modernism as a horrible example by which the whole movement is to be judged and condemned.

The theory of the modern designer consists very simply in the answering of a problem; whether the task be the painting of a picture, the design of a chair, the writing of a book, the result should be no other than an honest solution. The essential is clear thinking, unobstructed by preconceived notions. The processes are practically those of the engineer's acceptance of the problem, full analysis, decision as to type of result, and the use of the simplest forms to produce the required effect. The achievement, obviously, is not mechanical if the artist mastering the fundamentals has the genius and imagination to direct his creative ability. The difficulty in analyzing the modern is that the critic normally searches for familiar landmarks; not finding a comforting start, he finds it extremely difficult to forget the eccentricities of the individual and disdains high achievement in annoyance at the mental effort he himself must make to understand the work in question. Quite conceivably the mental restrictions of the critic are the barrier.

If real modernism consists of being alive, doing a job thoroughly by answering the problem in plan, material and design and not driving a new requirement into an old shell any honest designer must be a modernist.

. . .   1 9 3 0

ON THE DEVELOPMENT OF INDUSTRIAL BUILDINGS

PREACHING THE DOCTRINE of modernism has its entertaining reactions. A man believes that he himself sees the light and discovers that the beam he has noticed is merely a reflection of the illumination all about him. The moment he has acknowledged the existence of a point of view entirely at variance with that of a generation past, and in the architecture of the industrial building in particular, the result is sweeping. Where domestic work resists, grimly, the elimination of faked "quaintness," and where likewise the monumental building disdainfully avoids variation from precedent, the industrial structure sails merrily into experiment. Here common sense, the engineering instinct, cost, income, predominate. Beauty comes as a result of the solution of a problem where use of extraneous material or mere picturesqueness would be absurd.

It is evident that the new design of this type of structure dates from the first use of steel or reinforced lintels where large glass areas were possible. The curious factory structures with heavy brick walls and small windows are merely awaiting the pickaxe of tomorrow's demolition. Light and ventilation are paramount. The engineer smiles and suggests that the more modern conception would be that of purely scientific illumination by electricity; uniform distribution of the color and intensity of light required; ventilation to be effected by change of air at required intervals; the air itself to be regulated in moisture and temperature. Interesting theory, and very often essential in spite of the presence of windows which, though in some instances they may be of major importance, in others are permitted purely on sentimental allowance to the traditional instincts of employes who object to being shut off from a glimpse of what is occurring outside.

The industrial building is primarily and definitely a machine for the production of a commodity. The solutions to its problem can vary in material or detail, but, basically, the structure must answer its purpose. The column arrangement must fit properly the lines of machines, the receptacles for merchandise, the handling of goods for packing or shipping. There are, quite obviously, varying types of industrial structures that include the very tall factory buildings of New York, as well as the one-story, roof-lighted, shed type of mill that is found outside of the cities and on cheaper land. The tall buildings of the Garment Center in New York, the printing buildings developing in the Varick Street section and likewise in the forties east of Lexington Avenue, represent a characteristically large city type of factory. In New York, in particular, this type of structure has had intense development. Through real estate sales pressure, to a large extent, manufacturers have been brought together. The clothing trades, the silk, wool, leather, toy and furniture industries concentrate in definite districts where it is apparently convenient for the buyer to find his market and where the subsidiary businesses likewise cluster to avoid unnecessary loss of time in transacting their affairs. With this most persistent grouping there has come the problem of freight traffic,—the actual handling of the enormous quantities of goods of every nature. The clothing district in New York, for example, in turn attracts the various supply houses that handle fabrics,—silk, cotton, wool and rayon.

As the manufacturers find it difficult to conduct production on a large scale in locations where rents are relatively high and shipping conditions unfavorable, many of the large buildings develop into sales offices, finished stock rooms and executive offices, with the actual producing plants outside of the city or in sections of the New York area that are more adaptable. In the very tall New York factory structure, the standard of height has increased in the last ten years in a steadily rising scale. Where 16 floors was normal in 1920, 18 and 20 appeared later, until in this year monsters of 30 and more are commonplace. The results, considering the restrictions of zoning conditions for relatively small lots, develop large units of ground area and improved elevator and freight facilities.

The street traffic situation is one of the factors which will seriously endanger the steady growth of such districts. There is no question but that the manufacturer will presently object to the inconvenience of losing valuable time by the most absurd street congestion. The building can be as well planned as may be possible with modern facilities of every conceivable type, and yet if the moment the merchandise comes to the street, traffic is stopped, the building cannot be successful. The difficulty naturally has to do with an entirely unreasonable city plan,—narrow streets, intense through and cross circulation, and no direct arteries. The solution is yet to be found, though freight tunnels, secondary streets, may be less visionary when the actual demand insists on finding them.

The large buildings are highly specialized in equipment. The elevators and freight halls are designed to accommodate particular industries. Furniture, for example, requires large elevator cars in which bulky pieces can speedily be transferred; the floor loads are light. Millinery buildings require column arrangements adaptable to a number of small machines,—live steam for essential steps of manufacture; high ceilings for freight corridors because of the bulk of the cardboard boxes in which finished product is shipped. In other buildings the finished articles are handled mainly in express package form, so that provision must be made for express collecting and checking, independently of the constant entry of bulky raw material. In the design of these great units, low cost is naturally of major importance. Economy of plan and avoidance of areas that are poorly adapted to the uses intended, are paramount. Windows have to be arranged to provide sufficient light; the mechanical requirements as to live steam, electric power, ventilating shafts, package chutes are of importance.

In the factory building, high or low, column spacing seems to be the most important consideration. When the bays become too large, excess cost of columns and steel framing appears. Normal ceiling heights would likewise be affected by inordinately deep girders. In printing buildings the variation in sizes between heavy newspaper presses and the smaller types for normal printing of books and commercial production of every sort, determines the necessary clearance requirements, in walls and floor loads. Vibration under the stress of heavy machinery must be avoided by adequate load capacity and proper reinforcing.

The industrial structures' problem demands in the first instance an engineering solution. Areas conveniently disposed, adequate light, proper facilities for the transaction of the business in hand, are necessary. There can be no modernity in design that does not begin with such principles, and through such logical steps and the elimination of unnecessary decorative features it is possible that something new may develop. In fact, it is obvious that this must be the case, for every day's problem demands a new solution, whether it be the question of an aeroplane factory, a hangar, or a building for the handling of some new product that requires specific space, height, illumination. The major difficulty of the designer of industrial structures is that he is still conscious of the existence of an aesthetic problem. The untrained person, when he finishes what he considers a satisfactory solution of his practical problem, adds curious inserts of tile, bits of carving, or a mongrel door to satisfy some yearning for decoration. The fact that fine proportion, balance of mass, and agreeable color of material are more important, fails him.

1929

ON DECORATION AND ORNAMENT

THE DECORATIVE DETAILS that have been the stock in trade of workers in stone, plaster and wood are, after all, in a large measure, symbolic forms that are used indiscriminately and with a naive ignorance of style that should be surprising. The modeller for these materials has been accustomed to pick up the average blueprint and instinctively reach for his book of stock patterns. He may be working in French, Renaissance, Gothic, English Tudor, Moorish, anything in one day, and the pathetic note is that any originality might be crushed if the architect for whom he works be in a period mood. Decoration is a more precious thing than a mere assemblage of dead leaves, swags, bulls' heads and cartouches. It is primarily a desire to enrich a surface with a play of light and shade which should be accomplished by as careful modelling as would be required to complete a string of acanthus leaves. The decoration should not be the handiwork of a draughtsman but that of a sculptor, for there will be little use for pretty drawings. The scale and mass of the ornament will be delicate or coarse, in proportion to its proximity to the eye and be dependent on the material, whether bronze, stone, concrete, or brick.

The tall building on a comparatively narrow street in one of our big cities can no longer employ the decorative forms so lovingly and superbly handled by the masters of the past. Two reasons are evident; copying any man's work intended for a particular place or period is not only false but a stamp of inability in design; the detail, charming in a structure forty feet in height is ludicrous in one four hundred feet higher. If the detail, as much of the earlier American skyscraper architecture shows, is merely inflated to suit the increased distance from the eye the fallacy is no less obvious. One faces the fact, therefore, that the decoration of the tall building must produce the same agreeable effects of rhythm, symmetry, picturesqueness, sparkle, or whatever basic theories the designer wishes with quite new mediums. Flat surfaces take the place of the obsolete cornices and finally color in surfaces, in proportion to the distance from the observer, mark the accents that the artist desires.

Problems in decoration can no longer be handled by referring a designer to a given plate in a standard work. We have approached the situation where every factor of design must be analyzed primarily on a basis of its function, and then to its quality of interest. The artist will develop his personality through qualities in his own mind which make him different from his confrères. One man will enjoy the simple, flat, undecorated surfaces which are so characteristic of much of the modern architecture in Europe; another man will prefer the playfulness of form which demonstrates some whimsy or phantasy on his part.

The new attitude in design proceeds to consider decoration from a new angle. Decoration is not necessarily ornament. The interest of an object has primarily to do with its shape, proportion and color. The texture of its surface, the rhythms of the elements that break that surface either into planes or distinct areas of contrasting interest, becomes ornament.

1929

ON THE USE OF NEW MATERIALS

OUR AIM SHOULD BE to create, not so much a new form of design, but a decorative quality which can only be linked with the particular material involved. It is not so much a question of ignoring the past as facing the fact that we must look towards the future, and in this future, if our work is to remain, we also will produce works of art which are honest solutions of our problems and sincere expressions of our materials.

Under normal conditions of the modern day, the field is widespread, as far as choice of materials is concerned. With modern transportation means, every part of the world can contribute its woods, stones, or metals, in astounding variety. Where the architects of classic periods have limited themselves to the restrictions of local substances, the modern architect has squarely before him the demand for a thorough knowledge of his alphabet and the intelligence to use materials at hand in sympathy with his problems.

Our present period insists on one particular contribution. Science has made it possible to review, with considerable accuracy, the intellectual development of the past. The machine, facile transportation, an immense reservoir of materials of every conceivable type, lie before the designer. The scientist stands ready to produce new materials, obtain new results in finish, construction,—anything is possible to the architect. He can ignore the classic principle of the arch and its thrust, for he employs steel, reinforced concrete. If he chooses to build his wall of glass, of metal,—anything,—there is no longer an accepted formula. He can heat or chill, produce any variety of illumination, play with sound if he chooses, and what is not available today will be there tomorrow. What he cannot do is to ignore his epoch and be a complacent copyist, for *there* is death and ignominy.

One of the most injurious effects of the general practise of imitative design has been the blinding of designers to the functions of the objects they design and to the characteristics and ways of working the materials in which these objects are made. Designs that were made hundreds or thousands of years ago in accordance with the nature of the materials may be copied without any appreciation of the material on the part of the imitative designer. But satisfactory modern designs cannot be made without an intimate knowledge of the materials on the part of the designer, for without it he will very often run counter to the nature of his material and even more frequently fail to avail himself of the possibilities.

1 9 3 0

. . .

ON THE USE OF COLOR

THE PRACTICAL QUESTION of material, whether the effect will be produced in burnt clay or terra cotta, bricks covered with glazes baked under high temperatures, mosaic or glass, will depend, in large measure, on the ingenuity of the designers themselves. What seems to be particularly vital, however, is the conception of the use of color as a part of the structure and not as merely applied ornament. The possibilities of strong contrasts of colors, eliminating futile carving and the crockets, pinnacles and similar appendages of the early skyscraper, are unlimited. It will be found essential, however, for many essays of trial to determine what colors will maintain their values at particular heights and in prescribed locations, for even in the most carefully studied work the final effect has been proven to be quite at variance with what the original composition had suspected. The dream of a colored city, buildings in harmonious tones making great masses of beautiful pattern, may be less of a vision if the enterprising city developer suspects the result. There is evident economy of effort in the application of color in lieu of carved decoration that cannot be seen and the novelty of a structure that can be distinguished from its nondescript neighbors has a practical value that must appeal without question to the designer and his public. The precise manner of handling color, whether in masses, adapted as contrasts to the major tone of the building, as accents only, or where the entire structure develops color by reason of its basic material, depends again on the program of the creative designer. It is evident that a positive conception of the employment of color cannot countenance mere spots of bright tiles, marbles or other substances used to relieve the sobriety of a facade, although the individual, after he has experimented sufficiently, will quite promptly discover what media fit his taste and are adapted to the work he is doing; likewise the location, atmosphere and relative scale.

It would appear that the available materials for the application of color to our buildings have been greatly extended since man first erected shelters for his family and later for the housing of his works. It is questionable, however, if ever in history so little effort has been made to satisfy a normal satisfaction in the use of color. 1928

[24]

On New York ▪ Past, Present and Future

THE PRE-SETBACK building of dimension consisted of a box covered with some classic concoction, topped by a cornice of tin or terra cotta. Consider the Flatiron, the Tribune Tower, the World Building as notable shafts of a generation ago and find how little reason exists for most of their decoration and how feebly they stop. The cornice, once of stone and purporting to shed rain water from the face of the building, became a distorted and ridiculous affair of tin, copper, sheet iron, terra cotta, tied on with wires and merely lasting as a weak reminder of mere classicism. The setback régime sprang past them to a demand for some form of terminal on the upper surfaces of the various blocks; the painful processes of inspiration from the Gothic, Romanesque, Italian Renaissance, merely served to prove that the new Architecture required a new vocabulary. Receding surface instead of the flat wall, and requirements of large glass areas were details fitting in the new scheme; the housing of tanks, elevator rooms, roof penthouses of all sorts existed and these blocks demanded other forms than classic orders and balustrades. Gradually something evolved that was modern architecture, an exposition of the natural form required by the building of today.

The architectural characteristics which are indicative of our time are the rapid development within a few years of the plan, character and quality of these very buildings. In general, these characteristics are found in the greater usability of the plan and its adaptability to other and profitable changes in occupancy; in improved and more suitable general service which is conducive to the health and comfort of the occupants, the most important of which is adequate elevator equipment; and in the use of better, more durable and attractive structural materials. In the future larger rather than small buildings are inevitable in large urban centers, for they are more economical. The invention of a non-explosive motor fuel will allow the parking of all motor cars within the building, and provisions will be made for handling all freight and merchandise within buildings, removing the present sidewalk and street obstruction and traffic congestion. Real property will be assembled in large areas of one or more city blocks for large building units. These will be more uniform in appearance and economical in service. A keen competition and the demands of financiers will result in increased efficiency and adaptability of plan, a high standard of both external and internal appearance, and attractive lobbies and public spaces.

It is inevitable that architecture, which to the public consists principally of external appearance, will also keep step with the progress and more economical in service. A keen competition and the demands of function. After a survey of contemporary architecture throughout the country, it is obvious that this is the accepted basis of design,—it cannot be otherwise and possess the elements of progress and change.

Slowly, but surely, we are learning the fundamentals of the architecture of the new era.

This process is only in its inception, to be sure, though New York shows much that points the direction. There is no American decorative tradition and there is no particular reason why there should be one, considering our history and our population; although by this strange force of the practical, and due to quite hard-headed facts an American architecture will evolve that may clear the way for those who follow. In our experiments it may quite possibly take another generation to produce really great work, yet, the desire to be fresh and free is a symptom that together with active production must gather results.

1926

RESIDENCE OF MR. ELY JACQUES KAHN · ELMSFORD · NEW YORK

1 9 1 8

ZIMMERMAN SAXE AND
ZIMMERMAN - ASSOCIATED

BUILDING ON FIFTH AVENUE AT TWENTY-FIFTH STREET - NEW YORK CITY

1 9 1 9

JAY-THORPE BUILDING · 24 WEST FIFTY-SEVENTH STREET · NEW YORK CITY

1 9 2 1

HOSPITAL FOR JOINT DISEASES - MADISON AVENUE AT 123RD STREET - NEW YORK CITY
1 9 2 3

QUAKER RIDGE GOLF AND COUNTRY CLUB

QUAKER RIDGE - NEW YORK

1 9 2 4

DETAIL - ARSENAL BUILDING - NEW YORK CITY

ARSENAL BUILDING · SEVENTH AVENUE AT THIRTY-FIFTH STREET · NEW YORK CITY

1 9 2 5

550 SEVENTH AVENUE BUILDING - NEW YORK CITY

1 9 2 5

DETAIL - N. E. CORNER SIXTH AVENUE AND THIRTY-NINTH STREET - NEW YORK CITY
1 9 2 5

N. E. CORNER OF SIXTH AVENUE AND THIRTY-NINTH STREET · NEW YORK CITY

1 9 2 5

FURNITURE EXCHANGE BUILDING · LEXINGTON AVENUE AT THIRTY-SECOND STREET · NEW YORK CITY
1 9 2 6

DETAIL - FURNITURE EXCHANGE BUILDING

ENTRANCE DETAIL - FURNITURE EXCHANGE

DETAIL - N. W. CORNER SIXTH AVENUE AT THIRTY-SEVENTH STREET - NEW YORK CITY
1 9 2 6

N. W. CORNER SIXTH AVENUE AT THIRTY-SEVENTH STREET - NEW YORK CITY

1 9 2 6

625 SIXTH AVENUE BUILDING - NEW YORK CITY

1 9 2 6

DETAIL COURT SQUARE BUILDING - NEW YORK CITY

1 9 2 7

247 WEST THIRTY-FIFTH STREET -
NEW YORK CITY

1 9 2 7

ED. PINAUD FACTORY · 214 EAST TWENTY-FIRST STREET · NEW YORK CITY

1 9 2 7

INSURANCE CENTER BUILDING · 80 JOHN STREET · NEW YORK CITY

1 9 2 7

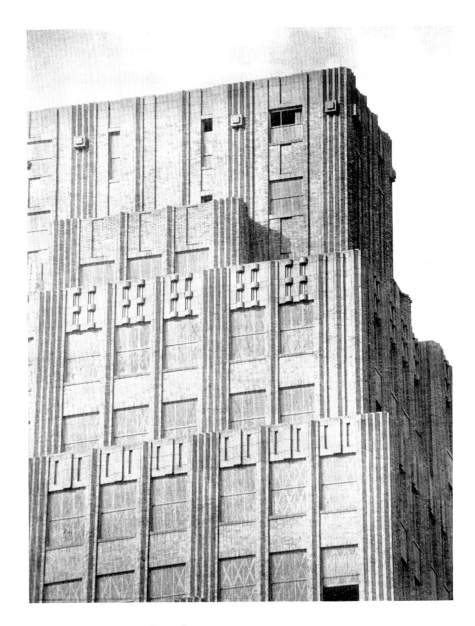

DETAIL - INTERNATIONAL TELEPHONE AND TELEGRAPH BUILDING
BROAD AND BEAVER STREETS - NEW YORK CITY

1   9   2   7

INTERNATIONAL TELEPHONE AND TELEGRAPH BUILDING · NEW YORK CITY

1 9 2 7

NUMBER TWO PARK AVENUE BUILDING · NEW YORK CITY

1 9 2 7

ENTRANCE VESTIBULE DETAILS - TWO PARK AVENUE

EXTERIOR DETAILS - TWO PARK AVENUE

DETAIL - PLASTER FRIEZE IN LOBBY - TWO PARK AVENUE - NEW YORK CITY
1 9 2 7

LOBBY DETAIL - NUMBER TWO PARK AVENUE BUILDING - NEW YORK CITY

1 9 2 7

BUILDING ON FIFTH AVENUE BETWEEN FIFTY-SEVENTH AND FIFTY-EIGHTH STREETS · NEW YORK CITY
1 9 2 7

DETAIL - SEVENTH AVENUE AT TWENTY-SIXTH STREET

ENTRANCE - SEVENTH AVENUE AT TWENTY-SIXTH STREET

BUILDING AT SEVENTH AVENUE AND TWENTY-SIXTH STREET - NEW YORK CITY

1 9 2 8

42-44 WEST THIRTY-NINTH STREET BUILDING · NEW YORK CITY

1 9 2 8

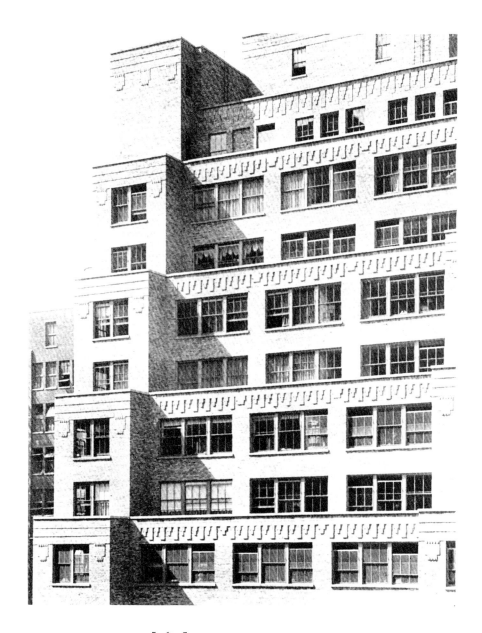

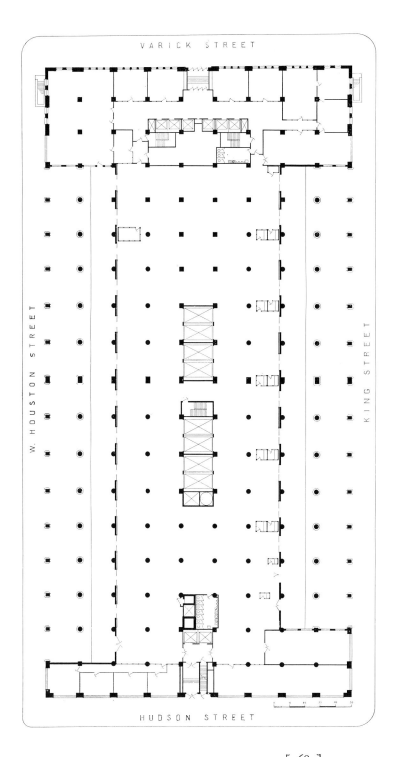

UNITED STATES APPRAISERS BUILDING - VARICK, KING AND HOUSTON STREETS - NEW YORK CITY

1 9 2 8

ENTRANCE DETAIL - UNITED STATES APPRAISERS BUILDING - NEW YORK CITY
1 9 2 8

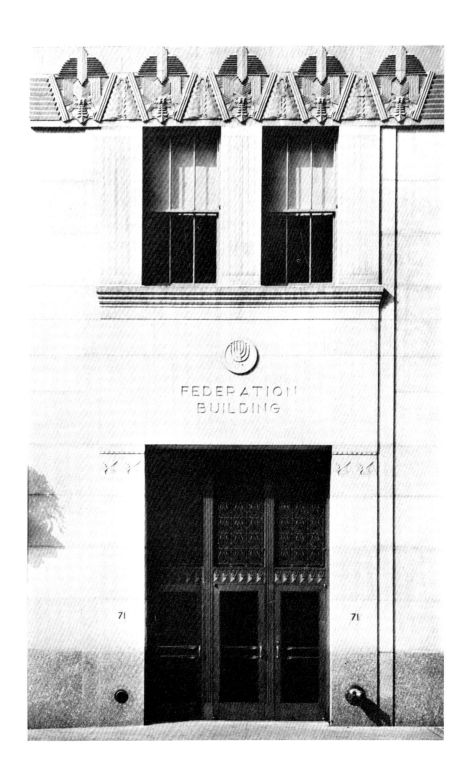

FEDERATION
BUILDING

ENTRANCE DETAIL · FEDERATION BUILDING · NEW YORK CITY

1 9 2 8

FILM CENTER BUILDING · NINTH AVENUE AT FORTY-FOURTH STREET · NEW YORK CITY
1 9 2 9

VESTIBULE DETAIL - FILM CENTER
NEW YORK CITY

FILM CENTER

ENTRANCE DETAIL - FILM CENTER
NEW YORK CITY

GARDEN SEAT AND TABLE · METROPOLITAN MUSEUM EXHIBIT   **NEW YORK CITY**

1 9 2 9

BATH AND DRESSING ROOM · METROPOLITAN MUSEUM EXHIBIT

NEW YORK CITY
1 9 2 9

S. E. CORNER BROADWAY AND FORTY-FIRST STREET · NEW YORK CITY
1 9 2 9

DETAIL - 111 JOHN STREET - NEW YORK CITY

ENTRANCE DETAIL - 111 JOHN STREET - NEW YORK CITY

INSURANCE BUILDING · 111 JOHN STREET · NEW YORK CITY

1 9 2 9

PORCH DETAIL · GLEN OAKS COUNTRY CLUB · GREAT NECK, L. I.
1 9 2 9

GLEN OAKS GOLF AND COUNTRY CLUB

530 SEVENTH AVENUE BUILDING · NEW YORK CITY

1 9 2 9

ALLIED ARTS BUILDING · 304 EAST FORTY-FIFTH STREET · NEW YORK CITY
1 9 2 9

ELEVATOR DOOR · 120 WALL STREET BUILDING · NEW YORK CITY

1 9 3 0

VIEW FROM EAST RIVER - 120 WALL STREET BUILDING - NEW YORK CITY

1 9 3 0

TYPICAL FLOOR PLAN - HOLLAND PLAZA BUILDING - NEW YORK CITY

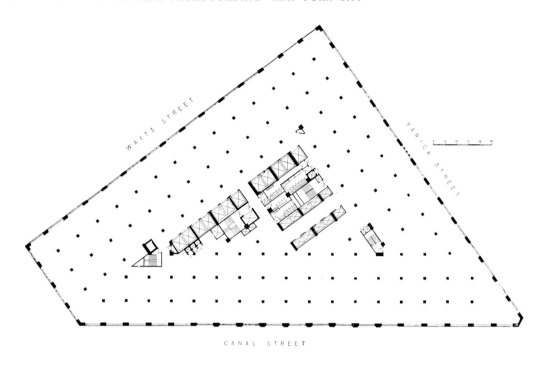

GROUND FLOOR PLAN - HOLLAND PLAZA BUILDING

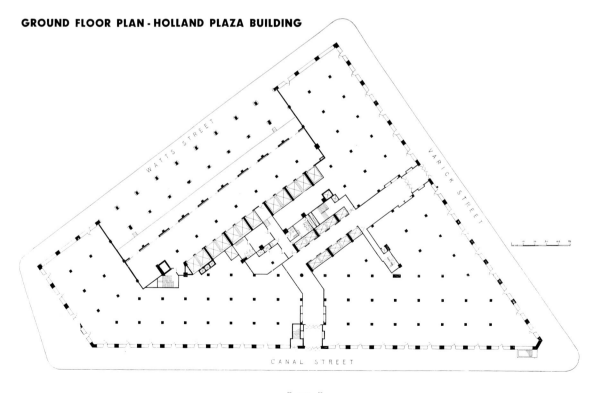

HOLLAND PLAZA BUILDING - CANAL, VARICK AND WATTS STREETS   -   NEW YORK CITY

1 9 3 0

LOBBY DETAIL - HOLLAND PLAZA BUILDING - NEW YORK CITY

1 9 3 0

SQUIBB BUILDING - 745 FIFTH AVENUE - NEW YORK CITY

1 9 3 0

ENTRANCE GRILLE - SQUIBB BUILDING - NEW YORK CITY
1 9 3 0

STAIR DETAIL - SQUIBB BUILDING - NEW YORK CITY

STAIR DETAIL - SQUIBB BUILDING - NEW YORK CITY

LIVING ROOM DETAIL - APARTMENT OF MRS. M. S. BENJAMIN - NEW YORK CITY
1 9 3 0

ENTRANCE VESTIBULE · EXECUTIVE OFFICES · E. R. SQUIBB & SONS · NEW YORK CITY

1 9 3 0

[99]

FIFTH AVENUE ENTRANCE - BONWIT TELLER - FIFTH AVENUE AT FIFTY-SIXTH STREET - NEW YORK CITY

1 9 3 0

GROUND FLOOR PLANS - 1400 AND 1410 BROADWAY BUILDINGS - NEW YORK CITY
1 9 3 1

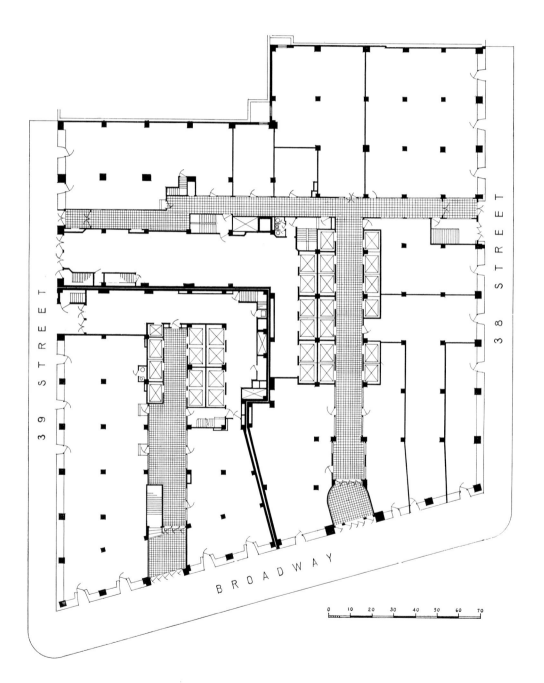

1400 AND 1410 BROADWAY BUILDINGS · NEW YORK CITY

1 9 3 1

VIEW FROM BRYANT PARK · 1400 AND 1410 BROADWAY BUILDINGS · NEW YORK CITY

1 9 3 1

DETAIL - ENTRANCE VESTIBULE - 1410 BROADWAY BUILDING - NEW YORK CITY

[107]

1 9 3 1

CONTINENTAL BUILDING · BROADWAY AT FORTY-FIRST STREET · NEW YORK CITY

1 9 3 1

RECEPTION ROOM - SECOND FLOOR - RICHARD HUDNUT BUILDING - NEW YORK CITY
1 9 3 1

RICHARD HUDNUT BUILDING · 693 FIFTH AVENUE · NEW YORK CITY

1 9 3 1

S. E. CORNER OF LEXINGTON AVENUE AND FIFTY-SEVENTH STREET - NEW YORK CITY

1 9 3 1

DETAIL · COMMERCE BUILDING · THIRD AVENUE AT FORTY-FOURTH STREET NEW YORK CITY
1 9 3 1

COMMERCE BUILDING - THIRD AVENUE AT FORTY-FOURTH STREET - NEW YORK CITY

1 9 3 1

LOBBY DETAIL - COMMERCE BUILDING - THIRD AVENUE AT FORTY-FOURTH STREET NEW YORK CITY
1 9 3 1

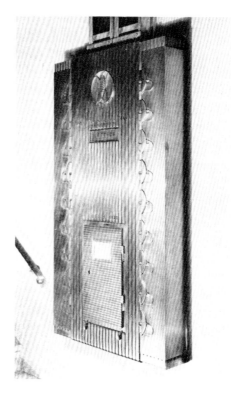

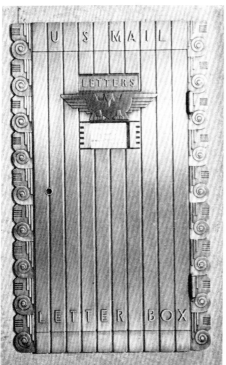

WALL STREET ENTRANCE - 120 WALL STREET BUILDING - NEW YORK CITY
1 9 3 0

ENTRANCE - HOLLAND PLAZA BUILDING
NEW YORK CITY

ENTRANCE - 259-263 FIFTH AVENUE
NEW YORK CITY

FABRIC DESIGN FOR THE SHELTON LOOMS

INDEX

ILLUSTRATIONS, *continued*

PHOTOGRAPHS BY SIGURD FISCHER

ENGRAVINGS BY KNAPP ENGRAVING COMPANY, INC.

BINDING BY EUGENE C. LEWIS COMPANY

DESIGNED AND PRINTED BY

PRINTING SERVICE CORPORATION

MCMXXXI